World War Two

500 Interesting Facts About Major Events, Battles, and People

Welcome Aboard, Check Out This Limited-Time Free Bonus!

Ahoy, reader! Welcome to the Ahoy Publications family, and thanks for snagging a copy of this book! Since you've chosen to join us on this journey, we'd like to offer you something special.

Check out the link below for a FREE e-book filled with delightful facts about American History.

But that's not all - you'll also have access to our exclusive email list with even more free e-books and insider knowledge. Well, what are ye waiting for? Visit the link below to join and set sail toward exciting adventures in American History.

To access your limited-time free bonus, go to: ahoypublications.com/

Table of Contents

Introduction 1

Invasion of Poland **(Sept. 1, 1939)** 2

The outbreak of World War Two **(Sept. 1, 1939)** 4

Germany Invades Scandinavia **(1940)** 6

Battle of Britain (July 10, 1940 – Oct. 31, 1940) 8

Attack on Pearl Harbor **(Dec. 7, 1941)** 10

Battle of Midway **(June 4, 1942 – June 7, 1942)** 12

Battle of Stalingrad **(Aug. 23, 1942 – Feb. 2, 1943)** 14

North Africa and Italy **(1940–1944)** 16

D-Day **(June 6, 1944)** 18

Battle of the Bulge **(Dec. 16, 1944 – Jan. 25, 1945)** 21

Battle of Berlin **(April 16, 1945 – May 2, 1945)** 23

V-E Day **(May 8, 1945)** 25

Potsdam Conference **(July 17, 1945 – Aug. 2, 1945)** 27

The Pacific Theater **(December 1941–September 1945)** 29

Atomic Bombings of Hiroshima and Nagasaki **(Aug. 6, 1945, Aug. 9, 1945)** 32

The Holocaust 34

Japanese American Internment 36

Weapons and Technologies 38

Women in World War Two 40

Resistance Movements 41

Legacies of World War Two 43

Formation of the United Nations **(Jan. 1, 1942)** 44

Post-war Reconstruction 46

Winston Churchill **(1874-1965)** 48

Joseph Stalin **(1878-1953)** 50

Franklin D. Roosevelt **(1882-1945)** 52

Benito Mussolini **(1883-1945)** 54

Adolf Hitler **(1889-1945)** 56

Hirohito **(1901-1989)** 58

Conclusion 60

Sources and Additional References 61

Introduction

From **the invasion of Poland in September 1939** to the **atomic bombings of Hiroshima and Nagasaki in August 1945**, World War Two was one of the most significant events in human history. In this book, we will explore how it changed our world forever.

Discover the stories of historical figures like **Adolf Hitler, Franklin D. Roosevelt, and Winston Churchill**, all of whom played a role in leading their countries during **World War Two**. Also, uncover events that don't get the spotlight, such as the internment of Japanese Americans and resistance efforts that have been largely forgotten over time.

You'll gain a deeper understanding of critical battles like **Operation Overlord** and **the Battle of Berlin.** Explore the strategies each side employed and their lasting impact on those involved.

We don't forget those who were affected either. This book talks about women, whose roles changed radically due to a lack of men in the workforce and survivors of **the Nazi** concentration camps and **the Holocaust.**

Finally, we will examine how post-war reconstruction occurred through **the declaration of the United Nations in 1942** and its first meeting in 1946, as well as the Potsdam Conference in 1945.

So, come with us on a journey as **we explore World War Two's** greatest leaders and those whose stories remain unsung yet equally as important.

Invasion of Poland
(Sept. 1st, 1939)

In 1939, Germany invaded Poland and sparked the start of World War II in Europe. This chapter will explore twenty facts about this invasion, which forever changed the course of history.

We'll discover how Nazi forces used tanks, aircraft, and artillery to attack Polish cities and how the Soviet Union attacked two weeks later. We'll also learn about the concentration camps the Germans set up and other atrocities committed during this period, including bombings that destroyed entire cities almost overnight.

1. On September 1st, 1939, Germany invaded Poland and started World War II in Europe.

2. Britain and France declared war on Germany and Russia after they invaded Poland without warning.

3. In late September 1940, Germany, Italy, and Japan allied to form the Axis powers.

4. Before invading Poland, Hitler signed a non-aggression pact with Stalin that allowed both countries to invade other territories without fear of being attacked by each other. It was known as the German-Soviet Pact or the Molotov–Ribbentrop Pact.

5. The Nazis used a new tactic called blitzkrieg or "lightning war" to attack from the east. The Soviet Union attacked from the east two weeks later, on September 17th.

6. The Polish Army was equipped with outdated weapons and equipment, making it difficult to compete against the more modern German forces.

7. The German forces alone inflicted nearly one million casualties on the Polish Armed Forces. Many Polish were taken prisoner during this invasion.

8. Many cities, including Warsaw, faced heavy bombing, which destroyed most buildings and left thousands homeless overnight.

9. As part of their strategy against Poland, **the Germans set up various concentration camps** where they imprisoned **Jews and Poles** who opposed German rule over the country. **Auschwitz,** located in southern Poland, is one such camp.

10. **During the invasion,** many **Jews living in Poland were rounded up into ghettos,** which were overcrowded areas of cities. They suffered mistreatment, disease, hunger, and despair. The ghettos were collection points for the Nazis to send people to death camps.

11. **German forces took over most of Poland by October 1939.** This is known as the **"Nazi-Soviet Occupation."**

12. **Germany annexed most of Poland and made it part of its empire.** They also set up a new state called **the General Government,** which was run by Hans Frank, a powerful Nazi official.

13. **The Polish government and military** fled the country, setting up opposition governments in exile in the UK and the USSR.

14. **The invasion led to thousands fleeing their homes**. Many went to neighboring countries, while others joined resistance groups that fought against German and Russian occupation.

15. **Resistance fighters** continued resisting Nazi rule even after Germany took control. Underground organizations such as **Armia Krajowa** (Home Army) provided support for guerrilla warfare and sabotage operations against the occupiers.

16. **During WWII,** there were multiple uprisings against Nazi occupiers. **The 1943 Warsaw Ghetto Uprising** was carried out by Polish Jews who refused to go to the camps. In 1944, Poles in Warsaw rose up against German rule again.

17. After the invasion, **Poland's borders were redrawn**, and new ones were established between Germany and the USSR. The Soviets proceeded to dominate Poland for over forty years.

18. Poland had been divided between the Germans and the Russians before, starting in 1772 and continuing in various forms from the 18th century until after WWI.

19. As part of **the Nazi-Soviet Pact**, some Polish territories were transferred to Lithuania, which also came under Soviet rule.

20. On **November 11th**, Poles commemorate those who were lost each year by celebrating a national holiday called **National Independence Day.**

The Outbreak of World War Two
(Sept. 1st, 1939)

Examine **how World War II in Europe was declared** and who was involved at the start of the war.

We'll learn how **alliances were formed between Britain and France** against the **Axis powers**. Let's discover twenty interesting facts about the outbreak of this world war.

21. **World War Two** was a war between two groups of countries, **the Allies** (led initially by Britain and France) and the **Axis powers** (led by Germany).

22. **The start of World War Two is usually seen as September 1st, 1939, when Germany invaded Poland.**

23. **It was the most destructive war in history**, with an estimated seventy million people killed or injured worldwide.

24. **Adolf Hitler was the leader of Nazi Germany during WWII.** He wanted to create a **German empire,** which led to conflicts with other nations like Britain and France.

25. **Hitler engineered the unification of Austria** in March 1938 to much acclaim in Germany and Austria.

26. After a series of peace talks in September 1938 at Munich, in which parts of **Czechoslovakia were given to Hitler,** Hitler moved into the rest of the country in March 1939.

27. **The Soviet Union signed a non-aggression pact with Nazi Germany in August 1939**, in which the two powers agreed to refrain from attacking each other.

28. **On September 3rd, Britain and France declared war on Germany** after Hitler refused to withdraw from Poland within two days. World War Two had officially started.

29. As soon as **the Germans invaded Poland**, they began implementing the anti-Semitic policies that would eventually lead to **the Holocaust.**

30. **The total cost of WWII is estimated to be around $1 trillion ($11 trillion today)**, making it the most expensive war ever fought. Most of that money was spent by or lent by the United States to its allies around the world.

31. Numerous technological advancements happened during the war, including **jet engines, radar systems, rockets/missiles, and the atomic bomb.**

32. **World War 2** also saw large-scale civilian resistance movements being formed to fight Nazi oppression.

33. **The Holocaust** was the mass killing of Jews that happened during WWII. **Nazi authorities systematically killed six million Jews and millions of other minorities,** such as Romani people, homosexuals, disabled persons, political dissidents, and Soviet prisoners, among others.

34. T**ens of millions of people in Europe were displaced** or forced into exile during WWII.

35. **The Second World War** brought about major changes to people's daily lives, such as food and gas rationing and increasing production levels for military equipment.

36. **Three European countries remained neutral during the war: Spain, Sweden, and Switzerland.** Spain had close relations with Hitler but refused to do more than send a few troops to fight. Switzerland remained solidly neutral. Despite trading natural resources with Hitler, Sweden leaned toward the Allies.

37. **Two of Hitler's allies were Hungary and Romania,** neither of which liked the other.

38. Before **the German invasion of the USSR, British Prime Minister Churchill** and others believed it was possible that the UK might have to fight Germany and the Soviet Union.

39. **Polish spies were responsible for sending a captured top-secret coding machine, the Enigma,** to England before Poland was defeated. This helped the British break many German codes during the war.

40. **Some Poles fled east to the Soviet Union.** Others fled south and then escaped to France and England. Polish forces under Soviet control fought with **the Red Army,** and Polish forces under Allied command fought with the British and Americans.

Germany Invades Scandinavia
(1940)

This chapter will explore the story of **Germany's invasion of Scandinavia during World War II.** We'll take a look at twenty fascinating facts about **Nazi occupation** and how it affected Denmark, Norway, and Sweden, both in terms of physical destruction and social upheaval.

We'll also uncover the legacy left behind by **German forces** when they finally withdrew from each country after their surrender in 1945, including memorials to fallen soldiers or monuments commemorating key battles between Allied forces against Nazi troops throughout **Scandinavia.**

41. **Hitler wanted to invade Denmark to cover Germany's northern flank.** He desired Norway because of its ports, long coastline, and mineral wealth.

42. At the time, **Norway** had one of Europe's largest merchant fleets, which helped provide a major source of income for its citizens. The Germans took these ships for themselves.

43. **Denmark and Norway were invaded on April 9th, 1940.**

44. **Adolf Hitler knew that he could control strong but neutral Sweden** if he conquered Denmark and Norway. Sweden was rich in mineral wealth.

45. **The Danish government decided not to resist** the invading Germans after they received an ultimatum demanding their surrender on April 9th, 1940. Denmark, whose army was small, knew it could win against the Germans.

46. **On April 9th, 1940, German troops began invading Norway** by air and sea simultaneously with landings in Norwegian cities and ports, including Oslo, Bergen, Trondheim, and Narvik.

47. **On April 10th, Norwegian Prime Minister Johan Nygaardsvold declared that Norway would defend itself against the German invasion.** His government was able to mobilize a large number of troops in just two days.

48. **A British-French force moved into Norway on April 14th** to help repel the Germans, but they were ultimately unsuccessful due to the size and strength of Germany's forces.

49. The **Norwegians eventually had to surrender on June 10th** after fighting bravely.

50.   **Resistance movements began in Denmark and Norway** not long after the Nazi victory.

51. **The invading German forces** seized control of all major ports and cities throughout Denmark and Norway. They also took key strategic locations, such as airfields, which they used to launch attacks on Britain.

52. **The Scandinavian countries** experienced social and political upheaval during their occupation by Nazi forces. They tried to maintain their culture while simultaneously being forced into compliance with German policies that restricted their freedoms.

53. **Sweden stayed neutral during the war** but was forced to make concessions to Germany to remain so. Sweden provided Germany with iron ore, steel, and other resources needed for the war effort.

54. **Norway and Denmark were occupied by the Nazis until the war in Europe ended in May 1945.**

55. Following WWII, t**he Scandinavian countries formed the Nordic Council** to promote cooperation through economic and military initiatives.

56. **The borders of Denmark and Norway remained the same at the end of the war.**

57. Both **Denmark and Norway joined NATO** in the years after WWII. **NATO** is a collective defense organization designed to protect its members from aggression, a lesson learned from WWII.

58. Some elements of **the original German invasion remain visible even today,** such as memorials for fallen soldiers or monuments honoring resistance fighters and victims of the German occupation.

59. As part of the rebuilding efforts, several international organizations were created to provide aid, including **the United Nations Relief and Rehabilitation Administration** (UNRRA) and its successor, **the International Refugee Organization** (IRO).

60. Today, **Germany, Denmark, and Norway are close political and military allies.**

Battle of Britain
(July 10th, 1940–Oct. 31st, 1940)

This chapter will explore **the incredible Battle of Britain**, which took place in 1940 after Hitler had taken Scandinavia, France, Holland, and Belgium. We'll take a look at twenty fascinating facts about this battle, including how it was fought mainly by **Allied and Axis air forces. Discover the aircraft used by both sides** and the heroic pilots who flew during this intense conflict. This battle also introduced **new technologies like radar systems and radio** jamming techniques to disrupt enemy communications. Furthermore, we'll discover why **Winston Churchill** referred to it in his famous speech about "The Few" and how women played an important role in helping ensure **victory for Britain.**

61. **The Battle of Britain** took place from the early summer to the late fall of 1940.

62. It was fought between **the German Luftwaffe** (air force) and the **British Royal Air Force** (RAF).

63. This battle marked the first time an **entire nation defended itself against an invasion using fighter aircraft.** No ground troops were used in combat, though the British Royal Navy played a role.

64. **The Battle of Britain** was one of the first major battles to be fought almost exclusively in the air. It changed how wars were fought forever.

65. The goal of the Germans was to gain control of British airspace so they could launch an invasion against Britain called **Operation Sea Lion.**

66. **On August 13th, or *Adlertag* ("Eagle Day")**, Germany sent many hundreds of aircraft on bombing raids against England.

67. Approximately **three thousand Allied pilots took part** in defending Great Britain during this battle, with over two-thirds of them being British citizens.

68. **Women played an important role during this battle**. For example, over one thousand female pilots called ATA or **"Air Transport Auxiliary"** ferried aircraft between airfields. Many other women took other military positions like radar operators, helping to provide essential information about incoming German raids. These women were called "WAAFs" for **"Women's Auxiliary Air Force."**

69. **During the battle, new technologies were used,** such as radar and improved radio systems that allowed RAF crews to be more effective at tracking down enemy planes.

70. **The Royal Air Force** also used new tactics, which are still studied today.

71. Fighter planes, such as **the Hawker Hurricane and Supermarine Spitfire,** were flown by British pilots who became national heroes for their bravery in battle.

72. Even though over **one thousand German aircraft were destroyed during the conflict,** they managed to destroy thousands of Allied airplanes.

73. Although **Germany had superior numbers during the battle,** British forces slowly but surely gained the upper hand, eventually **forcing Hitler to abandon his planned invasion.**

74. **The British victory in the Battle of Britain** saved England from German invasion.

75. **Had the Germans successfully invaded the UK,** the war might have lasted for many more years or ended in a settlement **that gave the Nazis control of Europe.**

76. **The Battle of Britain** was also a significant turning point in World War II since it was the first time Nazi Germany was stopped from achieving its goals.

77. **Winston Churchill famously talked about this battle, saying, "Never in the field of human conflict has so much been owed by so many to so few,"** referring to the brave RAF pilots who defended against overwhelming odds and helped save their nation.

78. After the war, a number of **German pilots served as instructors for future generations** of pilots from around the world, including Britain, the US, and at home in Germany.

79. **Many brave men and women received medals** for their service during this historic battle, including DFCs (Distinguished Flying Crosses), **DSOs** (Distinguished Service Orders), and **BEMs** (British Empire Medals).

80. In memory of those brave men and women who defended Great Britain during this epic battle, a memorial service is held every year at **Westminster Abbey on Battle of Britain Day (September 15th).**

Attack on Pearl Harbor
(Dec. 7th, 1941)

The attack on Pearl Harbor is one of the most significant events in American history. In 1941, **Japan launched a surprise attack on Naval Station Pearl Harbor in Hawaii,** which left more than 2,400 Americans dead and over 1,000 people injured. In this section, we take a look at twenty interesting facts about this historic event, including **how it led America into World War II.**

81. **The attack on Pearl Harbor happened on the morning of December 7th, 1941.**

82. **Japan attacked Pearl Harbor** without warning or declaration of war.

83. **Japan's aim in attacking Pearl Harbor** was to prevent US naval and naval air forces from interfering with its planned invasion of Southeast Asia, namely the countries of Thailand, Malaya **(today's Malaysia)**, and **the Philippines.** Unfortunately for the Japanese, their main targets, the US aircraft carriers, were not at Pearl Harbor on December 7th.

84. **More than 2,400 Americans died during the attack,** and over 1,000 people were injured.

85. **Eight battleships and three destroyers were sunk or badly damaged during the attack.**

86. **The battleship USS *Arizona*** was sunk during the battle. Its wreckage is still visible at Pearl Harbor today. Around 1**,175 sailors and Marines died on the *Arizona*.** Its memorial is hallowed ground.

87. **The surprise attack lasted just ninety minutes from start to finish.**

88. **American forces managed to shoot down twenty-nine Japanese planes** during the battle.

89. In a now-famous speech, **President Franklin Delano Roosevelt declared December 7th "a date which will live in infamy."** He asked Congress to declare war on Japan the next day.

90. **Men throughout America began flocking to recruiting centers while Roosevelt's speech** was being broadcast.

91. **Britain declared war on Japan on December 8th**, along with the French government in exile. On December 11th, **Hitler supported his Japanese ally by declaring war on the US.** From that point on, the US was at war in the Pacific and in Europe.

92. Following **the attack on Pearl Harbor, Japan quickly gained control** over much of Southeast Asia, including Malaya, Singapore, Indonesia, and New Guinea. Japan had already conquered parts of China in the 1930s. This led to tensions with the US since America was a close friend of China at the time.

93. By t**he spring of 1941, Japan's empire included** not only large parts of mainland Asia but also much of the western Pacific Ocean.

94. **The Japanese depended on their navy to ferry the army,** resupply their forces, and defend important areas.

95. During the war, **"Remember Pearl Harbor!"** was used as both a battle cry and a slogan to help recruitment.

96. In 1994, **President Bill Clinton declared December 7th "National Pearl Harbor Remembrance Day."**

97. **The USS *Arizona* Memorial** includes the sunken battleship and "black tears," which are made from oil that still leaks out of the ship into Pearl Harbor.

98. **The Japanese government** issued an official apology for attacking Pearl Harbor in 2010.

99. **After World War II ended, America became one of Japan's closest allies.** The two have strong economic and political ties today.

100. For many years, **survivors of the Pearl Harbor attack** would gather in Hawaii on December 7th.

The Battle of Midway
(June 4th-June 7th, 1942)

This chapter will explore **the Battle of Midway,** one of the most decisive battles in World War II. We'll take a look at twenty interesting facts about this battle and discover how it was an important **turning point in America's war efforts against Japan.**

101. **The Battle of Midway** was an extremely important battle in World War II **between the United States and Japan.**

102. **The battle lasted from June 4th to June 7th, 1942,** near a small island called Midway Atoll in the Pacific Ocean.

103. **Japan launched the Midway attack** so it could prevent the island from being used as a transport and supply station for US forces.

104. **If the Japanese took Midway Island,** which was a US territory, **they could block the US Navy** from entering the western Pacific.

105. **During this intense battle**, it's estimated that the **US lost over three hundred men,** although it inflicted many more casualties on the Japanese. **The Japanese lost over three thousand sailors and pilots.**

106. **The US had fewer ships and planes than Japan** but managed to win the battle.

107. **Seven aircraft carriers engaged in battle** during this conflict, making it the largest battle of its kind in history.

108. **The Japanese lost four of their aircraft carriers,** while only one American carrier was destroyed.

109. **The Japanese lost many experienced pilots in the battle**, which affected them for the rest of the war.

110. Right **after the first Japanese attack,** squadrons of US fighters launched waves of attacks with great accuracy, shooting down nearly 250 enemy airplanes while losing only about 30 in combat and another 100 or so on board **the sunken carrier USS *Lexington*.**

111. **This impressive victory is largely credited to the code-breaking done by American naval intelligence,** who were able to intercept and decipher Japanese radio messages.

112. **The victory at Midway was a turning point in World War II,** stopping Japan's expansion across the Pacific Ocean.

113. After this battle, **the US had a growing advantage over Japan** in technology, industry, and manpower.

114. **Admiral Chester Nimitz** was responsible for leading US forces during the Battle of Midway.

115. **Japan's navy was led by Isoroku Yamamoto.** He had studied in the United States for a time and liked America.

116. **Yamamoto was shot down by US forces in 1943** while moving from one base to another. American codebreakers discovered his schedule, and fighter planes were sent to shoot his plane down.

117. One of America's most renowned heroes during this battle was **US Navy Lieutenant George Gay.** He thought about crashing his plane into a Japanese ship but decided against it. He was the only one of his squadron to survive. He watched most of the battle while floating at sea.

118. **The Battle of Midway** is considered a turning point in naval history, as the battle marks when aircraft carriers became more important than battleships.

119. **Today, Midway Island is a memorial** and wildlife preserve.

120. In 1976 and 2019, **Hollywood movies were made** about this famous battle.

Battle of Stalingrad
(Aug. 23rd, 1942 – Feb. 2nd, 1943)

The Battle of Stalingrad was one of the most pivotal and devastating battles of World War II. This chapter will explore its fascinating history with twenty interesting facts. We'll discover how **over two million people were involved in the fight for control over Stalingrad**, resulting in a staggering number of casualties on both sides.

121. **Stalingrad** (now called **Volgograd**) is located in southern Russia, just east of Ukraine.

122. The battle lasted from August 23rd, 1942, to February 2nd, 1943, and **resulted in a Soviet victory over German forces.**

123. **Hungarian and Romanian troops** that were allied with the Germans also fought at Stalingrad.

124. Although **the battle began on August 23rd, 1942,** there is some confusion about its beginning because the German offensive on Stalingrad had begun as early as July 17th. Different sources may refer to either date when discussing the beginning of this pivotal battle.

125. **For five long months,** temperatures dropped far below zero degrees Celsius, making conditions even more difficult for the already weary fighters on both sides of the conflict.

126. **Tens of thousands of civilians died** from starvation, bombings, or in the fighting.

127. **The Germans lost 200,000 troops** in combat and an untold number of wounded. Of the ninety thousand men who went into Soviet prisoner-of-war camps, only five thousand ever returned home.

128. During this battle, legendary sniper duels took place between large numbers of Soviet and German snipers. **The most famous Soviet sniper was Vasily Zaitsev.**

129. **German forces were forced to surrender at Stalingrad** after their commander, **General Friedrich Paulus** (the highest-ranking German officer ever captured), decided to give up on February 2nd, 1943.

130. When **Adolf Hitler heard that his forces had been defeated at Stalingrad**, he refused to believe it. He had staked everything on winning.

131. **The Soviet victory over Germany at Stalingrad began a chain reaction** that eventually led to an Allied victory in 1945, ending World War II.

132. **Despite losing nearly 500,000 troops,** the Soviet victory at Stalingrad was the start of a successful counterattack against Nazi forces.

133. **The Battle of Stalingrad** marked a significant shift in how battles were fought, as it demonstrated that air power alone could not win a battle—something the Germans had tried to do by bombing the city into rubble.

134. **The Battle of Stalingrad** is also **famous for the intense close combat** that took place within the city.

135. Before WWII, **the Soviets renamed Tsaritsyn to "Stalingrad"** to honor their leader.

136. After the war, **the Soviet Union built a 279-foot-tall monument named *The Motherland Calls* in Stalingrad (today Volgograd).** The memorial is dedicated to those who lost their lives during the battle.

137. **In 2004, UNESCO declared Volgograd's Mamayev Kurgan a World Heritage Site.** It commemorates Soviet losses in Stalingrad.

138. **Mamayev Kurgan is a hill and likely an ancient burial site that overlooks the city.** It changed hands several times during the battle.

139. To this day, **the memorials and monuments in Volgograd** are some of the most visited sites in Russia.

140. The battle has been featured in many movies, including ***Stalingrad*** (1955 and remade in 1993), ***Enemy at the Gates*** (2001), and ***The Battle of Stalingrad*** (2005).

North Africa and Italy
(1940–1944)

World War II was fought in many different places, from the Arctic Circle to the deserts of North Africa to the "Eternal City" of Rome. In this section, you'll learn fifteen interesting facts from the often overlooked but critical **North African and Italian** campaigns.

141. **In 1935, Italian dictator Benito Mussolini attempted to restore what he called "the greatness of Rome"** by claiming territories in eastern and northern Africa. In 1936, Mussolini invaded one of the few independent countries in Africa, Ethiopia.

142. **The Ethiopians were led by Emperor Haile Selassie**. They were outgunned by the Italians in every way but put up a valiant fight. **Ethiopia eventually lost to the Italians,** who carried out a brutal but short occupation.

143. **In 1939, Mussolini took over the small southern European country of Albania,** which had been an Italian possession. It had achieved independence after WWI.

144. **In the fall of 1940, Mussolini attacked Greece but was handed a humiliating defeat.** The next spring, **Hitler** came to **Mussolini's** aid and attacked **Greece** after invading **Yugoslavia** to the north. The occupations of both Greece and Yugoslavia led to brutal guerilla wars against the Germans and Italians.

145. **In September 1940, Mussolini attempted to take over British-dominated Egypt,** hoping to capture the all-important Suez Canal. He was stopped and soon retreated across the North African desert along the coast of the southern Mediterranean Sea.

146. Hitler sent one of his best generals, **Erwin Rommel**, to North Africa with a force of tanks and infantry known as the **Afrika Korps**. Outnumbered but led with brilliance and skill, the Germans pushed the British and British Imperial forces (troops from Australia, New Zealand, and India) back across the Egyptian border.

147. For a year and a half, **Rommel and the British pushed each other back and forth across the desert** until British General Bernard Montgomery decisively defeated Rommel at the Second Battle of El Alamein.

148. **In late 1942, US forces invaded North Africa** from the west while British forces pushed the Axis forces from the east, resulting in Germany's defeat in North Africa.

149. **On July 10th, 1943, the Allies landed on the large southern Italian island of Sicily** and pushed the German and Italian forces back to the Italian mainland by July 25th.

150. **On July 24th, Mussolini was arrested by forces loyal to the king of Italy**. He was later rescued by German commandos in a daring raid but never led anything more than a small area in northern Italy after that.

151. **After the arrest of Mussolini, Hitler sent hundreds of thousands of troops to Italy to fight the Allies, taking German troops that were fighting against the Soviet Union.**

152. The Allies were divided on the importance of invading Italy, but British Prime Minister **Winston Churchill** insisted that Germany could be entered from the south, ending the war. This was one of his biggest mistakes in the war. When the war ended in 1945, Allied troops were still fighting in Italy.

153. The most famous of the many pitched and rugged battles that took place in Italy was at **Monte Cassino**, a mountaintop monastery overlooking the road to Rome. **Monte Cassino was a victory for the Allies**, but it was extremely costly and controversial.

154. **Rome was liberated on June 5th, 1944, by US forces,** one day before the famous **D-Day landings in France.**

155. **Many Italians joined the fight against the Germans.** Many paid the ultimate price for trying to free their country from tyranny.

D-Day
(June 6th, 1944)

This chapter will explore **the monumental events of D-Day in 1944.**
We'll take a look at twenty fascinating facts about one of **history's most significant military operations: Operation Overlord.** Discover how this momentous battle gave the Allies a decisive victory in WWII and ultimately **helped bring an end to Nazi Germany's reign of terror.**

156. **D-Day was the largest seaborne invasion in history, with over 150,000 troops** crossing the English Channel to land on the beaches of Normandy on more than 5,000 ships.

157. **The invasion was part of Operation Overlord**, which lasted from **June 6th to August 25th, 1944.** D-Day happened on June 6th.

158. **The soldiers were part of eleven Allied nations,** including Britain, Canada, and the US.

159. **Between five and seven thousand ships were used by Allied forces** to carry troops across the English Channel to the beaches of Normandy on D-Day.

160. **During Operation Overlord, soldiers used amphibious tanks, which allowed them to move from water onto land,** and specialized landing craft designed for transporting infantry across short distances quickly and safely.

161. **The battle had three main objectives: secure a foothold on French** soil by capturing key towns and cities, such as Caen and Cherbourg; **expand the foothold** with a push southward to take Paris; **and secure the whole of France** by pushing eastward into Germany. **All of these goals were achieved,** but the operation got behind schedule due to stiff German resistance.

162. **The operation was so large that it required extensive planning and coordination among the Allies.** Code names were even given to each beachhead to keep the landing areas secret.

163. **The code name Operation Overlord** was chosen because it sounded like something from Greek mythology, hinting at the importance of its mission.

164. **The BBC broadcasted a coded message during its 9 p.m. news bulletin on June 5th, 1944,** warning the French Resistance near the coast that an invasion was imminent. This is sometimes known as the **"Longest Day" broadcast.**

165. **Operation Overlord began at midnight** when British glider pilots landed behind German lines to destroy bridges and cut off German communication routes during their attack on France's Normandy region.

166. **The US 82nd and 101st Airborne Divisions parachuted behind enemy lines** in the early morning of June 6th to disrupt German defenses preparing for the Allied attack on Normandy's beaches.

167. **More than twenty-four thousand US, British, and Canadian paratroopers were dropped close to their objectives** despite heavy anti-aircraft fire from German forces below. The Germans had been alerted ahead of time that an invasion was likely.

168. Around 7:30 a.m., Allied forces started landing at five different beachheads along a fifty-mile stretch of coastline in northern France: **Utah** Beach, **Omaha** Beach, **Gold** Beach, **Juno** Beach, and **Sword** Beach.

169. **By June 11th, all five beachheads were secured,** which allowed thousands more troops to come ashore as **part of Operation Overlord.** This included many more tanks, artillery pieces, and other equipment needed for future battles against Nazi Germany's forces.

170. **In total, there were over 425,000 casualties,** including those killed or wounded, in just under two months of fighting in Normandy.

171. **On D-Day alone, the British and Canadians lost around 1,000 soldiers**, while **the Americans suffered around 2,500** casualties. Most American combat deaths took place on Omaha Beach.

172. **The success of Operation Overlord was a major turning point in World War II,** as the Allies now had control over the Western Front and could launch more attacks against Hitler's forces from this position.

173. **After weeks of fierce fighting in Normandy, Paris was liberated by Allied troops on August 25ᵗʰ, 1944.** This marked the end of Operation Overlord and a major victory for the Allies in WWII.

174. In remembrance of those who gave their lives fighting for freedom during WWII, **an annual ceremony is held at Normandy American Cemetery.**

175. **On June 6ᵗʰ, 2019, France commemorated seventy-five years since D-Day with special events,** such as flyovers by military aircraft and displays honoring veterans that had served in World War Two.

Battle of the Bulge
(Dec. 16th, 1944 – Jan. 25th, 1945)

Discover **the incredible story of the Battle of the Bulge, one of World War II's most iconic battles.** In this chapter, we will examine twenty interesting facts about this remarkable conflict that took place mainly **between German and American troops.**

176. **"The Bulge" took place mostly in the Ardennes region of France and Belgium,** along the border between Germany and its occupied territories.

177. **The Battle of the Bulge** was also called **the Ardennes Counteroffensive by US forces** or *Wacht am Rhein* (Watch on the Rhine) **by German forces.**

178. It is thought that **Hitler's plan in launching the attack was an attempt to split up Allied forces** so he could negotiate a peace agreement for more favorable terms.

179. The battle is sometimes referred to as **"Hitler's Last Gamble"** due to its failed attempts at negotiating peace through force.

180. **It was the biggest battle fought by the United States in World War II,** with close to a million soldiers involved on both sides of the conflict at some point during the battle.

181. Many of the **US troops** initially stationed in **the Ardennes** when the battle began were raw replacements who hadn't seen combat. Some held the Germans up with stubborn fighting, but **the biggest surrender of US combat troops in history** took place at the start of the battle.

182. **The German army attacked through Belgium's Ardennes Forest,** which was thought to be too difficult to defend against an attack due to its rough terrain and dense forest areas.

183. **The Germans initially succeeded in taking several towns** but were stopped at Bastogne by US troops until reinforcements from **General George S. Patton's** Third Army division arrived and repelled their advance after heavy losses on both sides.

184. Before being stopped at Bastogne on January 25th, 1945, **German troops had managed to advance about ninety miles into Allied lines,** making it one of the longest retreats in American military history.

185. **For the first few days of the battle, bad weather prevented US planes from attacking the Germans** and resupplying US troops on the ground.

186. **The weather was freezing**, with temperatures reaching **as low as -20°C**, leading to many soldiers suffering from frostbite.

187. **More men were taken off the front lines from frostbite than combat wounds.**

188. **The American forces suffered around 75,000 casualties,** while **German losses were estimated to be over 100,000 men killed or captured.**

189. Many famous people served during the battle, such as **General George S Patton** and the famous **Easy Company** of *Band of Brothers* fame.

190. **Despite heavy losses on both sides,** it marked a major turning point in the war since it was **the last major offensive from German forces** and began the final phase to defeat Hitler.

191. **Twenty Medals of Honor** were awarded during this battle, including three posthumous awards given to those who lost their lives **while performing heroic acts** that saved many other soldiers during this conflict.

192. **General Dwight D Eisenhower** thought he was the target of a German assassination squad and remained in hiding for part of the battle.

193. **The Battle of the Bulge helped to hasten the end of World War II** since it showed that Germany was no longer able to mount significant offensives.

194. **In 1965, a memorial was built at Luxembourg American Cemetery located near Hamm, Luxembourg,** honoring over five thousand US soldiers who died during this battle.

195. **For years, veterans gathered every year at luxury resorts,** such as Hotel des Ardennes, for a reunion commemorating their service and sacrifice during the Battle of the Bulge.

Battle of Berlin
(April 16th—May 2nd, 1945)

This chapter will explore twenty interesting facts about this monumental battle that saw **the Soviets capture the German capital,** ending the war and marking a new era for Europe. We'll uncover details on the number of soldiers that fought, as well as **Adolf Hitler's fate**.

196. **The Battle of Berlin was the final battle of World War II in Europe.**

197. The battle lasted **from April 16th, 1945, to May 2nd, 1945.**

198. **Berlin was mostly in ruins before the battle even began,** as the British and Americans had been bombing the city for years.

199. **The Soviets surrounded the city and attacked from all sides.**

200. While **the Soviets were pushing into Germany from the east, the Western Allies** (Britain and the US) **advanced from the west.**

201. **Nearly 2.5 million Red Army troops and approximately 700,000 Germans fought in Berlin** and its suburbs.

202. Although there are no exact numbers available, it is estimated that between **seventy-five thousand and eighty thousand Red Army soldiers died in this battle.** Some figures go much higher.

203. **Nearly three million German soldiers were taken captive by Allied forces** between D-Day and the end of the war.

204. **Over 100,000 civilians died** in the battle due to bombing and fighting in the streets.

205. The amount of **firepower the Red Army used in Berlin** exceeded the weight of the bombs dropped on the city by the Western Allies throughout the war.

206. **Much of the city was destroyed** by British and American bombing and the Soviet assault.

207. Many famous landmarks, such as **Brandenburg Gate and the Reichstag** (parliament) **building, were heavily damaged.**

208. After the war, **many Soviet soldiers claimed to have been the one to raise the Soviet flag over the Reichstag,** but the famous photograph taken near the end of the battle was likely posed.

209. **Adolf Hitler committed suicide by shooting himself. His new wife, Eva Braun, took poison.** Their bodies were burned outside of his bunker.

210. **Admiral Karl Doenitz was named chancellor** after the death of Hitler. He held the position for just a few days.

211. Many leading Nazi officials, including Hermann Göring, **Heinrich Himmler,** and **Albert Speer**, were arrested by Allied forces.

212. **Himmler committed suicide shortly after being captured.**

213. **After the Battle of Berlin, many German scientists were taken to the US and the USSR** to research space exploration and rocket engineering.

214. **On May 7th, 1945, official surrender papers were signed by German forces**. The war officially ended at 12:01 a.m. on May 8th.

215. **The Soviets celebrated their victory with a massive military parade on June 24th, 1945, in Moscow.**

V-E Day
(May 8th, 1945)

This chapter will explore **V-E Day (Victory in Europe Day)**, which marks **the day Nazi Germany surrendered.** We'll take a look at twenty interesting facts about the celebration, from huge parades to moments of silence honoring those who had lost their lives.

216. **V-E Day stands for "Victory in Europe Day"** and marks **the day Nazi Germany surrendered** during World War II.

217. At one point, **Hitler controlled almost all of Europe,** a big part of North Africa, and a large part of the Soviet Union.

218. People from all of the occupied countries pitched in to defeat **Hitler.** However, we must not forget that **many collaborated with the Nazis** too.

219. It was estimated that over **seventy million people died during the war.** Most of them were civilians.

220. **Germany's official surrender document was signed on May 7th, 1945,** but it wasn't until May 8th that it became public knowledge.

221. In the United States, **President Harry Truman declared May 8th, 1945, a national holiday.**

222. **On V-E Day, millions of people gathered in streets** throughout Europe, North America, and elsewhere to celebrate with flags and banners.

223. **Ships and their crews also joined in celebrating,** with horns blowing loudly in port city around the world.

224. People throughout America celebrated by flying flags from their homes and businesses.

225. Many US cities held parades with marching bands playing patriotic songs like **"God Bless America."**

226. In London, over ten thousand people marched to Buckingham Palace to see the royal family and Britain's hero of the war, **Prime Minister Winston Churchill.**

227. At 3 p.m., King George VI made a historic radio address to announce victory had been achieved.

228. People celebrated by having street parties filled with singing, dancing, and drinking throughout Britain.

229. In Britain, Prime Minister Winston Churchill made a victory speech that was broadcast on the radio to millions around the world.

230. Red, white, and blue (which are the colors of both Great Britain and the US) bunting hung from windows along city streets while people sang songs like **"God Save the King."**

231. Many famous landmarks were lit up or draped in cloth, such as in **Trafalgar Square,** where **Nelson's Column** stood proudly surrounded by thousands of cheering citizens.

232. The flags of all three major Allied Nations (the **US**, the **UK**, and the **USSR**) waved from rooftops in cities across Europe as a symbol of **the Allied victory over Nazi Germany.**

233. On V-E Day, people celebrated by singing and dancing but also took time to remember those who lost their lives during World War II by honoring them with moments of silence.

234. After V-E Day, the focus shifted to defeating **Japan.**

235. Within a very short time, the three major powers (the US and the UK on one side and the USSR on the other) became adversaries in a **new type of conflict called the Cold War.**

The Potsdam Conference
(July 17th–Aug. 2nd, 1945)

Explore the fascinating **history of the Potsdam Conference**. This chapter will examine twenty interesting facts about **the historic meeting between leaders** from three countries—**the United States, Britain, and the Soviet Union**. Discover their discussion of **Europe's postwar future** after World War II ended.

236. The Potsdam Conference was a meeting between the leaders of three major Allied countries: **the United States, Britain, and the Soviet Union.**

237. The meeting marks one of only three times that the leaders of **the US, USSR, and Britain** were together at once, with the other two being the **Tehran Conference (1943)** and **the Yalta Conference (1945)**.

238. The Potsdam Conference took place in July and August **1945 in Potsdam, Germany**, near Berlin.

239. US President Harry Truman, British Prime Ministers Winston Churchill and his successor, Clement Attlee, and **Soviet Premier Joseph Stalin** attended this important conference to discuss Europe's postwar future.

240. They decided to divide Germany into four occupation zones, one for each country plus France.

241. They also talked about plans to restore peace throughout Europe by establishing new governments in Nazi-occupied European countries.

242. Other topics included reparations from Germany, punishment of war criminals, expelling German people from other parts of Eastern Europe, and setting up international organizations such as **the United Nations (UN).**

243. During the conference, **Churchill lost his reelection in Britain.** Despite being a hero to the British people, most believed Labor Party leader Clement Attlee would be a better peacetime prime minister.

244. Potsdam was **President Truman's first appearance on the international stage. President Franklin D. Roosevelt,** the longest-serving president in US history, **died in April 1945.**

245. **On July 24ᵗʰ, 1945, US President Truman received news of the successful atomic bomb test** in New Mexico, giving him more leverage during the negotiations.

246. **The Potsdam Declaration was signed on August 2ⁿᵈ, 1945,** setting out terms for Japan's unconditional surrender. The declaration warned Japan that it would face "prompt and utter destruction" if it did not surrender.

247. **Shortly after the conference ended, an atomic bomb was dropped by US forces on Hiroshima, Japan,** on August 6ᵗʰ, followed by another one **three days later on Nagasaki.**

248. This conference marked a turning point in history, as it **created new boundaries between countries,** many of which remain today.

249. **Germany was partitioned at the end of the war into two countries:** democratic **West Germany,** also known as the Federal Republic of Germany, and communist **East Germany,** also known as the Democratic Republic of Germany.

250. **At the start of the war in 1939, Britain was considered a "great power."** By 1945, its power was dwarfed by the US and the Soviet Union.

251. **The Soviets promised free elections** in all of the territories in Eastern Europe under their control. Elections happened, but they were rigged. **Communist regimes took power in Soviet-controlled areas.**

252. Although **peace was maintained in Europe,** conversations at Potsdam and in other conferences made it clear that **the relationship between the West and the USSR was going to be difficult.**

253. **The Cold War** was a political and economic struggle **between the democratic US and the communist USSR.** Although the two never fought each other in a direct conflict, they did fight on opposing sides in proxy wars.

254. **The Cold War lasted from 1945 until 1991** when the Soviet Union was dismantled.

255. **At the time, it wasn't clear if peace would last,** but today, we can reflect on the Potsdam Conference as a success in international relations.

The Pacific Theater
(December 1941–September 1945)

The war in the Pacific was fought mainly **between the forces of the United States and those of Japan,** but British, Australian, Indian, and Dutch forces fought in the Pacific theater as well. **The war in the Pacific was fought on land, sea, and air,** with the Allies pushing the Japanese back across the water toward their home islands. Let's explore eighteen facts about this part of World War II.

256. **The Japanese invasion of China in 1936 is considered by many historians to be the unofficial beginning of WWII.** The invasion lasted from 1936 to 1945. Millions of Chinese lives were lost, with most of them being civilian deaths.

257. **America had a good relationship with China at the time.** Once the Japanese took over French territories in Southeast Asia, **the United States imposed a trade embargo on Japan.** The most important things Japan bought from the US were things they didn't have enough of at home, such as oil and steel.

258. **Japanese leaders believed that a war with the US was inevitable** but knew they likely couldn't win a long war against the richest country in the world. They planned a lightning offensive, which they hoped would scare the US into peace talks.

259. **A crucial part of the Japanese plan was attacking the US naval port and air station at Pearl Harbor, Hawaii.** The main target of the attack was to be the US aircraft carriers, but when **the attack happened on December 7th, 1941,** the carriers were out at sea. Still, the Japanese attack sunk and damaged US battleships and other warships and claimed over two thousand lives.

260. **The next day, President Roosevelt asked Congress to declare war on Japan,** calling the attack on Pearl Harbor "an unprovoked and dastardly attack."

261. At the same time **the attack on Pearl Harbor** was happening, **the Japanese invaded a number of US and British possessions in Asia**, most importantly the Philippines and Singapore.

262. **US and Filipino troops defended the Philippines bravely** but were outnumbered. When they surrendered, they were subject to brutal treatment by the Japanese.

263. American military commander and governor of the Philippines, **Douglas MacArthur,** vowed, "I will return." He did after leading the southern advance of US troops back across the Pacific. **The Philippines was liberated in 1945.**

264. **America's plan was to launch a two-pronged attack across the Pacific.** The US Navy would transport and support the Marine Corps in a drive through the central Pacific and the US Army through the southwestern Pacific.

265. **The Marines fought some of the most famous WWII battles in the Pacific.** The first major battle there was fought by the Marines and the US Army on **the island of Guadalcanal,** east of Australia. Guadalcanal was the first land victory for the Allies in the Pacific.

266. **In early June 1942, US and Japanese naval forces clashed near the island of Midway,** resulting in a one-sided American victory. Midway was the turning point of the war in the Pacific.

267. As the war went on, the difference between the Japanese and American economies became clear in many ways. **The Americans outproduced the Japanese in nearly every way** as far as ships, tanks, and planes were concerned. It's also estimated that, on average, each US soldier had almost one ton of supplies behind him in support, while the Japanese had about fifty pounds.

268. The outgunned and outmanned Japanese put up a tremendously stiff defense. For most of the war, **virtually no Japanese soldiers were taken prisoner.** They either made suicidal charges or killed themselves in the bunkers and cave systems they had fortified.

269. Some of the more **famous battles of WWII** that the US was part of took place in the Pacific. **These battles include Tarawa, Peleliu, Saipan, Iwo Jima** (the site of the famous flag-raising photo), and **Okinawa.**

270. By early 1944, **the Americans dominated the Pacific,** though the Japanese made a number of desperate attempts to change that, including the **famous Battle of the Leyte Gulf** and in the seas around Okinawa, where waves of **"kamikaze"** suicide pilots dove their planes into American ships or died trying.

271. While American troops were preparing themselves for a costly invasion of Japan, it was announced **the US had dropped the first atomic bomb on Hiroshima on August 6th, 1945. A second bomb was dropped on Nagasaki on August 9th.** Shortly thereafter, the Japanese surrendered, ending WWII in Asia and the Pacific.

272. **In the last days of the war, the Soviet Union invaded Japanese-held territories in China,** forcing millions of Japanese troops to surrender to them and to Chinese forces that had been supplied by the US and Great Britain.

273. **From 1945 to the present day, Japan has been one of America's most dependable allies.** However, until very recently, the Japanese forces were not permitted to be used overseas in anything but a humanitarian capacity.

The Atomic Bombings of Hiroshima and Nagasaki

This chapter will explore the devastating **atomic bombings of Hiroshima and Nagasaki.** We'll take a look at twenty interesting facts about these tragedies, including their impact on those affected by them and how they are remembered today.

We'll also discover the **immense power behind these bombs** and the damage they caused.

274. **On August 6ᵗʰ, 1945, the United States dropped an atomic bomb on Hiroshima in Japan.**

275. The name of the atomic bomb was "Little Boy."

276. Three days later, **another atomic bomb called "Fat Man" was dropped on Nagasaki in Japan.**

277. Estimates vary, but **at least 200,000 people were killed by these bombs** immediately or died within a few months due to radiation sickness and other injuries.

278. **Many of the children of these survivors were affected by radiation.** Cancer rates in Hiroshima and Nagasaki went up after the war.

279. **It is estimated that around one million Japanese people were injured by both bombings.**

280. **Thousands of pets also died during these events** due to radiation poisoning and other injuries caused by the explosions.

281. **Radiation poisoning from the bombings still causes health problems for survivors today.** These survivors are known as *hibakusha* (atomic-bomb-affected people).

282. The heat generated from these **bombs reached temperatures hotter than the sun's surface.**

283. **The Hiroshima bomb** had an explosive **power of fifteen thousand tons of TNT.**

284. Many buildings near ground zero disintegrated. Intense firestorms stormed across both cities, destroying many buildings.

285. The mushroom clouds released during each bombing could be seen fifty miles away.

286. These two bombings are widely credited with ending World War II.

287. As of April 2023, the US has been the only country to use atomic bombs in war.

288. The US president at the time of the bombings was Harry Truman. Today, some criticize his actions.

289. In 1946, the US established the Atomic Bomb Casualty Commission for bomb-affected survivors in Japan.

290. Hiroshima and Nagasaki are popular tourist destinations today. Many visit memorials to pay respect to the victims of the bombings.

291. The Hiroshima Peace Memorial includes the former Hiroshima Prefectural Industrial Promotion Hall, which stands as a shell, just as it did after the bombing of the city.

292. Some surviving *hibakusha* became world-renowned activists for peace and nuclear arms reduction.

293. Each year, memorial services are held in Hiroshima and Nagasaki to commemorate those who died in the bombings.

The Holocaust

The Holocaust was a period in history marked by immense suffering and tragedy. **Starting in 1933, the Nazis began to persecute people** for a variety of reasons, mainly their religion or race. **Jews were the Nazis' biggest target.**

The Holocaust ultimately resulted in the death of at least six million European Jews and millions of other minorities. Let's take a look at fifteen interesting facts about this dark time in history.

294. **Holocaust** means **"destruction" in Greek**. The Hebrew word for the Holocaust is **Shoah**, which means **"catastrophe."**

295. **The term "Holocaust" was first used in the mid-1950s** when people started learning more about this tragic event from survivors and Nazi documents.

296. **The Holocaust lasted from 1933 to 1945.** People, especially Jews, were persecuted by the Nazis because of their religion, race, or other differences.

297. **About six million Jews and perhaps five million others, including Soviet prisoners of war, the Roma, homosexuals, and disabled people, were killed by the Nazis and their collaborators.**

298. **Adolf Hitler, the leader of Nazi Germany, wanted to create a "pure" German populace** with no Jews or other minorities.

299. Many **concentration camps**, such as **Dachau, Buchenwald,** and **Mauthausen,** were built in Europe. Prisoners were housed and worked there.

300. **The prisoners lived in harsh conditions.** Many perished from diseases, starvation, exhaustion, or gas chambers used for mass murder purposes.

301. **Adolf Eichmann was one of the main architects behind organizing** deportations of Jews from various European countries into ghettos. He also helped to organize the rail system that transported Jews directly to death camps like **Auschwitz- Birkenau.**

302. **Many non-Jewish people risked their lives by helping Jews escape** capture or providing food.

303. **Anne Frank wrote an autobiographical diary while she hid with her family from Nazis** before being discovered and sent to a concentration camp. **She died at the Bergen-Belsen camp** about a month before it was liberated.

304. **SS doctors in the camps subjected prisoners to inhumane experimentations,** most of which had no real scientific value.

305. **After World War II ended in 1945, survivors started sharing their heartbreaking stories** about life inside these camps. Their stories shocked the world at large and helped to create awareness against racial and religious discrimination.

306. Many memorials were built around the world as an act of remembrance for those who lost their lives during the Holocaust. The most sacred of these is at **Yad Vashem, Israel.**

307. **The United Nations declared January 27th International Holocaust Remembrance Day.** It is dedicated to remembering victims of this tragedy worldwide every year. **January 27th** is the day the Auschwitz-Birkenau extermination camp was liberated by the Red Army.

308. **Today, education is vital in making sure we never forget what happened during the Holocaust** so history won't repeat itself.

Japanese American Internment

The Japanese American internment marks a dark and difficult period in US history Over 120,000 people of Japanese ancestry were forced to leave their homes and live in special camps set up by the government against their will. This chapter examines twenty facts about this event, from its causes to its consequences.

309. **On February 19ᵗʰ, 1942, President Franklin D. Roosevelt issued Executive Order 9066,** which allowed military commanders to designate any area of the country as off-limits from certain groups. This order was used to create **the Japanese American internment camps.**

310. The US government thought that some **Japanese Americans and Japanese immigrants would be a threat to national security during World War II,** so they put them in these camps.

311. Most of **those who were interned were US citizens** or permanent residents of California, Oregon, Washington State, and Alaska. Not all of them had connections with Japan.

312. **Japanese Americans from Hawaii were not interned.** The islands were isolated. More importantly, the Japanese American community there was important for the island's agricultural output.

313. **The internment camps** were, for the most part, located in remote areas of California, Arizona, Idaho, Utah, Wyoming, and Arkansas.

314. **Families often only had one suitcase each** when they left for the camp, and many lost everything they owned because it was sold by the government at auction for rock-bottom prices while they were away.

315. Many **non-Japanese Americans believed internment was a good thing.** Others were indifferent. Some purchased Japanese-American property and returned it to its owners after the war.

316. **People living in the internment camps lived together in barracks** surrounded by barbed wire fences and armed guards. There was almost no privacy or freedom inside the camp walls.

317. **The internees had some rights,** like free speech, but weren't allowed to leave the camps without permission.

318. **Internees helped build roads and other infrastructure at many of these camps.** Others worked on farms or factories that had been set up within camp walls. Some earned money doing this work, but not everyone did, so living conditions were often difficult.

319. **The camps had schools and stores** for things like magazines, cigarettes, and other simple items. However, prices were higher than they would have been outside of the camp walls. Food was provided, though it was not to many people's tastes and often did not come in sufficient quantities.

320. **People inside the camps** tried to maintain a sense of normalcy by forming clubs, sports teams, and even newspapers.

321. **During World War II, many internees volunteered for military service** despite their families being held in internment camps; some even became decorated war heroes.

322. **The 100th Infantry Battalion and the 442nd Regiment were made up of Japanese Americans from Hawaii** and the internment camps. They were two of the most highly decorated combat units in American history.

323. **Some Japanese Americans became translators during the war in the Pacific** and played an especially important role toward the end of the war when they talked more and more Japanese into surrendering rather than committing suicide.

324. **Many internees showed great courage during their time in camps** by speaking out against racism or standing up for what they believed was right, even when faced with danger or discrimination. **These acts of bravery inspired future generations.**

325. **Today, the Japanese American internment is seen as a dark chapter in US history.** The government had no real evidence that any of these people were a threat to national security, yet they were still treated unfairly and put into camps.

326. **Decades later, the US government apologized for putting Japanese Americans into these concentration-like camps.**

327. **In 1988, President Ronald Reagan** provided payments or "redress" (money) to those who were interned in these camps or their descendants. This is known as **the Civil Liberties Act.**

328. **Japanese American internment** is an example of **discrimination against minorities,** something that still happens today. Today, many civil rights groups work to protect minority communities from unfair treatment.

World War Two Weapons and Technologies

This chapter will take an in-depth look into **the fascinating weapons and technologies developed during World War Two.** We'll explore nineteen interesting facts about the new technologies employed by both sides of the conflict, from **rocket** propulsion to **radar detection** to **atomic bombs.**

329. **During World War Two, rocket technology was used for the first time in warfare.**

330. **The V-1 flying bomb** (or **"buzz bomb"**) was an early type of cruise missile **developed during WWII**. It had no pilot but used guidance systems instead. These weapons caused destruction wherever they landed.

331. **The atomic bombs dropped on Hiroshima and Nagasaki** were the deadliest weapons ever created in history.

332. The most widely produced single type of aircraft of WWII was the German **Messerschmitt Bf 109 fighter plane**. Over thirty-five thousand were built!

333. **The US and British had machine guns mounted underneath planes** to shoot down enemy aircraft approaching from below.

334. **Paratroopers were soldiers who jumped out of planes and parachuted into battle,** often behind enemy lines, to surprise their opponents. **WWII saw the first use of these troops.**

335. **The Allies had air superiority for most of the war,** which meant they were able to bomb German cities with planes like the **B-17 Flying Fortress bomber.**

336. **Submarines were commonly used during WWII** to transport supplies and attack enemy ships. Specialized anti-submarine surface vessels and planes hunted them down.

337. **SONAR ("Sound and Navigation Ranging")** was developed by the Allies during WWII to help hunt enemy submarines.

338. **Radar technology** allowed armies and air forces to detect incoming aircraft from miles away, giving them a decided advantage. **RADAR ("Radio Detection and Ranging")** was first employed by the Allies but was employed by Germany shortly after.

339. **Unlike WWI, countries did not use poison gas on the battlefield during WWII.**

340. **Tanks were developed in WWI but didn't reach their full potential until WWII.** The main US tank was called the **Sherman** after Civil War **General William Tecumseh Sherman.**

341. **Man-carried flame throwers** were developed during WWI but were used on tanks and other vehicles during WWII.

342. **The German MG-42 was the best machine gun of WWII,** and its descendants are still being used by armies around the world today.

343. **The US developed a proximity fuse for its artillery shells,** which allowed troops to set the altitude the shells would go off in the air. This was more deadly than when they exploded after hitting the ground.

344. **The shaped charge was developed during WWII,** which allowed shells to penetrate tanks and other armored vehicles more easily.

345. **Militaries around the world developed new types of camouflage** to better hide troops and equipment.

346. **The Enigma machine allowed German military personnel to encode their messages** so that only people with a special key could read what it said. This made it harder for Allied code-breakers to intercept their communications, but the Allies were eventually able to break the code. **The scientific advances of WWII marked the beginning of great changes** and innovations in military technology.

Women in World War Two

This chapter will explore **the incredible contributions of women during World War Two.** We'll discover nine amazing facts about their involvement in military and non-combat roles, from **working as secret agents to flying planes** for various air forces.

347. During World War Two, **many women served in the military,** working as nurses, pilots, mechanics, spies, and more.

348. During World War Two, **some Japanese women served as nurses for their country's troops**. A few even flew planes. However, Japanese society at the time greatly limited what women could and could not do.

349. About **four hundred British women were recruited by the Special Operations** Executive during WWII, many of whom became **secret agents behind enemy lines.**

350. **The Women's Auxiliary Air Force** (WAAF) was created in 1939 to help Britain's Royal Air Force with non-combat duties, such as radar operators or air traffic controllers. American women joined **the Women's Army Corps** (WAC), which allowed them to serve their country in a variety of non-combat duties.

351. **Over five hundred female pilots flew planes for a program called WASP** (Women Airforce Service Pilots) during WWII. These women flew planes from factories to staging areas on the coasts, allowing more men to fly in war zones.

352. **More than six million US women entered the workforce during WWII** and took on jobs traditionally done by men. These jobs included roles like electricians and welders at factories producing supplies for troops overseas.

353. **In 1941, the Australian government enlisted** over twenty-seven thousand women into an **all-female volunteer force known as WAAAF** (Women's Auxiliary Australian Air Force), which helped support pilots flying combat missions during WWII.

354. **The Soviet Union had one of the highest levels of female participation in combat forces during WWII, with around 800,000 Russian women serving in active duty at any time.** Many Soviet women fought on the front lines as infantry, snipers, tank crew, and pilots.

355. **Tens of thousands of women** from many Allied countries and territories **served as nurses during the war.**

World War Two Resistance Movements

This chapter will explore the brave and inspiring **history of resistance movements during World War Two.**

We'll uncover eleven interesting facts about how people across Europe used bravery and ingenuity **to sabotage enemy operations** and **fight against** oppressive governments.

356. **During World War 2**, many people around the world **formed resistance movements to fight against Nazi and Japanese occupiers** and collaborationist governments.

357. **Resistance fighters used their courage, skills,** and ingenuity to sabotage enemy operations and help the Allied forces win the war.

358. **Some famous examples of WWII resistance groups** include the **French** Resistance, the **Polish** Home Army, **Yugoslav** Partisans, the **Greek** People's Liberation Army, **Dutch** NSB (National Socialist Movement), and **Danish** Freedom Fighters.

359. **In France, roughly 250,000 to 500,000 people were members of active resistance movements.** Hundreds of thousands provided logistical support, such as hiding weapons or **providing food and shelter for fugitives, including Allied pilots** who had been shot down behind enemy lines.

360. **Much of the Norwegian population was involved with some type of secret activity** that supported Allied troops during World War Two on both sides of the border between Sweden and Norway.

361. **The White Rose group was an anti-Nazi student organization based at Munich University.** Its members engaged in acts of non-violent resistance against the Nazi regime. Almost all of the group paid for their resistance with their lives.

362. **The earliest official American resistance group was called the Office of Strategic Services** (OSS), which was established on June 13th, 1942, by **President Franklin D. Roosevelt** to collect and analyze strategic information during WWII.

363. **In Poland, the Home Army** was a large underground army formed in 1942 consisting mostly of volunteers from different backgrounds. **They fought against German forces** for five years until 1945.

364. **Jewish resistance fighters organized several armed uprisings across Europe,** including in the **Vilna Ghetto** in **Lithuania** and the **Warsaw Ghetto**. These brave men and women put their lives at risk while fighting off heavily armed Nazi soldiers with little more than homemade weapons, such as **Molotov cocktails and handguns.**

365. **Most of the men, women, and children** who took part in the uprisings in **ghettos** perished in the fighting or in the concentration camps.

366. **During World War Two, many women played an important role in the Resistance movement** as spies or couriers, delivering secret messages between various safehouses located all over Europe.

The Legacy of World War Two

This chapter will explore **the legacy of World War Two,** an event that had a profound impact on the world. We'll take a look at eleven interesting facts about its **devastating effects and how it changed global power dynamics** and led to advances in technology.

367. **World War Two involved many countries** from all over the world, mostly from Europe and Asia.

368. **More than seventy million people lost their lives** during World War Two—more than any other war in history.

369. **The end of World War Two marked a major shift in global power.** The United States and the Soviet Union were the two most powerful countries in the world when the war ended.

370. **After WWII**, new international organizations were created, such as **the United Nations (UN)** and **the International Monetary Fund (IMF).** These organizations still promote peace and economic stability around the world.

371. **Many different countries were affected by WWII.** For instance, Poland's borders were redrawn. India gained independence. Korea was divided in two. And Germany was divided into East and West until 1989.

372. **The nation of Israel was founded in 1948.** Many Holocaust survivors helped establish the "new" country.

373. **Several countries were given independence after WWII,** such as India, the Philippines, and Indonesia, which had all previously been under British, American, or Dutch rule, respectively.

374. **Many refugees sought safety outside their home** countries due to the political turmoil caused by WWII. Some of these people remained in their new countries for many reasons, chiefly because of economic opportunities or political repression in their home countries.

375. **The atomic bombs ended WWII** and left lasting effects on the environment. The radiation from the bombs caused birth defects and high cancer rates in Japan for quite some time.

376. After the war, **German jet and rocket technology** led directly to the exploration of space.

377. Despite the fact that many wars have been fought since **WWII**, there has not been a **global conflict** since **1945.**

Formation of the United Nations
(Jan. 1st, 1942)

This chapter will explore the history of one of the most influential international organizations on Earth: **the United Nations.** We'll take a look at eighteen interesting facts about its formation, leaders, goals, and more!

378. **Allied nations from around the world** announced their intention to join a **"United Nations"** after the war on **January 1st, 1942.**

379. **The United Nations (UN)** is an international organization that aims to **promote peace and security around the world.**

380. **In 1945, when the UN was established,** there were fifty-one countries involved in the organization.

381. In **1945, the fifty-one member countries created the Charter of the United Nations,** which outlines how decisions would be made by using consensus-based voting procedures.

382. **The UN's first session was held on April 25th** of that same year when representatives met **in San Francisco** to sign an agreement forming this new international body.

383. **The first secretary-general** of the United Nations was **Norwegian** politican **Trygve Lie** (in off. 1946–1953).

384. **The United Nations adopted the Universal Declaration of Human Rights in 1948,** which sets out basic rights that everyone should have no matter where they live.

385. Every year, the world celebrates **International Day of Peace on September 21st.** This date marks when the member states first joined together to form the UN in 1945.

386. **Today, the UN has 193 member countries** from all over the world.

387. **The UN headquarters are in New York City, USA,** but the organization also has offices in Geneva, Vienna, Nairobi, and elsewhere.

388. **The official languages used by the UN** are Arabic, Mandarin Chinese, English, French, Russian, and Spanish.

389. **The UN is made up of six main parts:** the General Assembly, the Security Council, the Economic and Social Council, the Trusteeship Council Secretariat, and the International Court of Justice.

390. **The United Nations Security Council is one of the six principal organs of the United Nations.** It is charged with maintaining international peace and security, accepting new members to the United Nations, and approving any changes to its charter.

391. **The Security Council has fifteen members,** consisting of five veto-wielding permanent members **(the People's Republic of China, France, Russia, the UK, and the US)** and ten elected non-permanent members that serve two-year terms.

392. **The UN also has many specialized agencies,** such as **UNESCO** (the United Nations Educational Scientific Cultural Organization), which promotes cultural understanding worldwide.

393. **Every year since 1979, people around the world have taken part in World Food Day on October 16ᵗʰ.** This day commemorates the founding of the Food and Agriculture Organization **(FAO)**, which is part of the UN.

394. **The UN also works to combat climate change, end hunger, and provide humanitarian aid** when disasters strike around the world.

395. **The official flag of the United Nations shows a map of the world with two olive branches surrounding it,** symbolizing peace on our planet.

Post-World War Two Reconstruction

Following the end of World War Two in 1945, many countries faced a monumental task: rebuilding their cities and economies. In this chapter, we will explore **the post-WWII reconstruction period,** looking at eleven interesting facts about how governments and international organizations **worked together to help bring stability back to Europe** and other parts of the world.

396. **After World War Two ended in 1945, many countries had to rebuild their cities and economies.**

397. **Postwar reconstruction focused on rebuilding infrastructure across Europe**, such as bridges, roads, and railways, connecting communities once more. Countries also worked to promote trade.

398. **After WWII, efforts were made by different governments** to provide more educational opportunities for their citizens in the hope that they would lead to a better and more peaceful future.

399. **The United Nations was formed after WWII** to help keep peace worldwide and promote economic development.

400. **In 1945, the United Nations Relief and Rehabilitation Administration (UNRRA)** was set up to support refugees who had been displaced due to WWII or persecution from Nazi Germany.

401. **The European Coal and Steel Community was founded** in 1952 to help promote economic cooperation between the countries of Western Europe.

402. The Treaty of Rome (1957) created the European Economic Community (EEC), which eventually became known as **the European Union (EU)**. This organization is focused on fostering closer ties and trade agreements among its member states.

403. In Europe, **the US Marshall Plan** (named after George Marshall, overall US commander during WWII and secretary of state afterward) **provided $13 billion in financial aid from 1948 to 1951 to help rebuild European nations** devastated by WWII warfare.

404. **The Marshall Plan played another important role—preventing the rise of communism in Western Europe.**

405. **The Berlin Airlift of 1948 helped deliver supplies** like food and fuel into West Berlin when it became blockaded by Soviet forces during the Cold War.

406. **In Japan, a new constitution was adopted,** which included pacifist principles, such as renouncing war forever. This marked a major change from its militaristic past. The **Japanese Constitution was written by American General Douglas MacArthur's** staff, and most of it is still in place today.

Winston Churchill
(1874–1965)

This chapter will **explore the life and legacy of Winston Churchill,** Britain's most revered **prime minister.**

We'll take a look at sixteen facts about his inspiring leadership during World War Two, including his strong alliance with US President Franklin D. Roosevelt and some lesser-known stories.

407. **Winston Churchill was the prime minister of the United Kingdom during World War Two.**

408. **He was born on November 30th, 1874,** in Oxfordshire, England.

409. **In 1940, he became one of the first world leaders to order evacuations from cities** threatened by bombs dropped from planes, which saved many lives.

410. **During his early years as prime minister,** Britain had success with its navy, defeating Italy's ships at Cape Matapan in 1941 and sinking the German battleship *Bismarck* in May 1941.

411. **Under Churchill's leadership, British troops** helped win decisive victories over Germany at El Alamein (1942) and in Italy.

412. **In 1941, he inadvertently launched the "V for Victory" campaign,** where people used their fingers to make a V sign, showing their determination to win the war.

413. **Churchill also boosted morale among troops by visiting them** on many occasions, including Christmas Day in France in 1944.

414. **Churchill and US President Franklin D. Roosevelt met many times during the war.** Churchill actually stayed at the White House for a number of weeks during the conflict.

415. **At the end of WWII, Churchill helped shape the postwar world with his Iron Curtain speech,** warning against Soviet expansionism.

416. **During the WWII period alone, Churchill received over two hundred medals** and orders of honor throughout Europe and America, which was a truly remarkable feat.

417. **In 1953, Winston Churchill was awarded the Nobel Prize for Literature,** recognizing his writings on history, politics, and military strategy during wartime.

418. **Churchill lost the prime ministership in 1945 but regained it in 1952.**

419. **He retired in 1955 but remained active in public life until the last years of his life.**

420. **His funeral procession drew over one million Londoners,** and dignitaries from all around the world came to pay tribute to him.

421. **Churchill is remembered today as Britain's greatest prime minister and was voted as the "greatest Briton of all time" by the British people** in a 1970 poll. To put that in perspective, British history is over two thousand years old.

422. **In 1963, the United States made Winston Churchill an honorary citizen of the country.** At the time, only Marquis de Lafayette, the Frenchman who helped the colonists during the American Revolution, had been given that honor.

Joseph Stalin
(1878–1953)

This chapter will explore the life and times of **Joseph Stalin, one of the most influential figures in history.**

From his rise to power as **the ruler of the Soviet Union in 1922 until he died in 1953,** we'll look at fifteen interesting facts about how he helped shape World War II and its aftermath.

423. **Joseph Stalin was the leader of the Soviet Union from 1922 until he died in 1953.**

424. **During WWII, he formed alliances with many countries** the Soviet Union had previously been hostile to.

425. **He signed a non-aggression pact with Nazi Germany shortly before the invasion of Poland.** This gave Stalin time to prepare Russia's defenses while gaining territory from other countries like Finland, eastern Poland, and the Baltic states in 1939 and 1940.

426. **In 1941, after Hitler broke the 1939 non-aggression pact, Stalin declared war against him** and ordered Russian troops into battle against German forces in what is known as the Great Patriotic War.

427. **Stalin worked closely with British Prime Minister Winston Churchill and US President Franklin D. Roosevelt during WWII as part of the "Big Three."**

428. **The Soviet Union had one of the largest armies in WWII** (over twelve million soldiers).

429. **At first, Stalin took direct command of all Soviet forces in the war** but soon realized he was over his head and appointed competent generals like Zhukov, Konev, and Rokossovsky.

430. **During WWII, he oversaw military production efforts that helped Russia survive and eventually win against Germany's forces.** Some say this was even more important than fighting on the battlefield.

431. **Stalin worked closely with partisan groups within German-occupied territories** who fought back against Nazi rule by using guerrilla warfare tactics, such as sabotage and assassination.

432. **During the war, he sought to increase the USSR's power by taking over much of Eastern Europe** through military force or diplomacy once Nazi Germany had been defeated, a process known as Sovietization.

433. **By 1944, most of Eastern Europe was occupied by Soviet forces.** These lands would not be free again until 1991, when the Soviet Union fell.

434. **Stalin's forces entered Berlin in 1945,** marking the war's end for the European theater.

435. **Stalin made sure there were no internal rebellions during the war** by sending dissidents to prison camps known as gulags.

436. **Stalin is thought to have been responsible for the deaths of millions of people due to his brutal tactics and purges,** including those killed at home during World War II.

437. **Stalin insisted that many of the Soviet "republics" be given individual nation status in the UN** after WWII, giving him added votes.

Franklin D. Roosevelt
(1882–1945)

This chapter will explore the remarkable life and career of **Franklin D. Roosevelt, the thirty-second president of the United States.**

We'll take a look at sixteen interesting facts about his presidency and how he led America through **World War Two.**

438. Franklin D. Roosevelt was the thirty-second president of the United States, **serving from 1933 to 1945.**

439. In 1944, he became the only US president ever elected four times when he won his fourth term in office with running mate Harry S. Truman.

440. He was a Democrat and led America through most of World War Two.

441. During the Great Depression, Roosevelt began programs like **Social Security and the Works Progress Administration** (WPA).

442. FDR asked Congress to declare war on Japan shortly after the attack on Pearl Harbor.

443. Roosevelt worked closely with British Prime Minister Winston Churchill in helping to plan the Allied invasion of Nazi-occupied Europe known as Operation Overlord or D-Day.

444. FDR helped draw up the Atlantic Charter with British Prime Minister Winston Churchill in 1941 to promote global cooperation and human rights after WWII ended.

445. In 1941, he created the Lend-Lease program, which allowed Britain and other Allied nations to borrow military supplies from the US during WWII without having to pay for them upfront in exchange for British bases in the Western Hemisphere.

446. **He also helped create a new international organization called the United Nations (UN)** after WWII ended in 1945. The organization seeks global cooperation on peacekeeping efforts around the world.

447. **FDR helped create a new global financial system after WWII, known as the Bretton Woods Agreement in 1944,** and established **the International Monetary Fund (IMF)** and the World Bank Organization for economic stability between nations.

448. **FDR gave one of his famous speeches, known as "The Four Freedoms," on January 6th, 1941,** where he outlined four essential human freedoms that everyone should be entitled to: freedom of speech and expression, freedom of worship, freedom from want, and freedom from fear.

449. **First Lady Eleanor Roosevelt played an important role during the war,** helping to raise both money and awareness.

450. **FDR was the first president to travel by airplane while in office and made many trips abroad during WWII** to meet with Allied leaders like Winston Churchill, Joseph Stalin, Charles de Gaulle, and Chiang Kai-shek.

451. **He also attended two international summits with Stalin and Churchill during WWII,** famously called the Tehran Conference (1943) and **the Yalta Conference (1945).**

452. **He died days before the Battle of Berlin** broke out due to health complications.

453. **Millions of people worldwide mourned the loss of FDR when he died** from a massive stroke on April 12th, 1945.

Benito Mussolini
(1883–1945)

This chapter will explore **the life and legacy of Benito Mussolini,** one of the most notorious figures in modern history. We will take a look at sixteen interesting facts about **his rise to power and Italy's occupations in Ethiopia and Albania.**

454. **Benito Mussolini was an Italian leader who came to power in 1922,** becoming the first fascist ruler in Europe.

455. **He started as a journalist and socialist politician** before leading **Italy as prime minister from 1922 until his downfall in 1943.**

456. **In 1919, he created the Fascist Party**, which had strong ideas about controlling citizens' lives through government force or threats.

457. **He believed in a dictatorship**, which meant he wanted all the power and authority in one person or group (like himself). **This person or group would lead Italy as a single-party state** free of any opposition groups or individuals that disagreed.

458. **Mussolini's nickname was** *Il Duce*, meaning **"The Leader,"** which many people used when addressing him directly or referring to him publicly.

459. **Before WWII, Mussolini formed militarized organizations known as "Blackshirts"** to enforce his will.

460. **During his time as prime minister, Mussolini is said to have been responsible for the deaths of around 300,000 people** due to forced labor camps he created, deportations, or executions.

461. **Ethiopia became part of Italian East Africa after Mussolini invaded and conquered it in 1936. He also annexed Albania in 1940.**

462. **Mussolini was a close ally of Hitler,** whom he met personally many times before and during the war.

463. **In 1943, the Allied invasion of Sicily led to a revolt against Mussolini in the Italian government.** He was arrested. He was rescued in a daring raid by German commandos but was apprehended again toward the end of the war.

464. **Italy fought alongside Nazi Germany and Japan during World War Two.**

465. **Mussolini's mistress, Clara Petacci, was captured with him.**

466. **Mussolini and his mistress were executed by firing squad on April 28th, 1945,** at the age of sixty-one. His body was hung upside down from a meat hook for public display in **Milan's Piazzale Loreto,** where twenty-five anti-fascists had been shot three years earlier.

467. **Mussolini had three sons** named **Vittorio** (born 1916), **Bruno** (born 1918), and **Romano** (born 1927). He trained them to be ready to take over after his death, but he was killed before they could assume power.

468. **Sadly, fascism is still alive in Italy,** though to a much smaller degree than during WWII.

469. **After WWII ended, many countries adopted "anti-fascist" policies that rejected the principles of fascism,** such as dictatorship or total control over citizens' lives.

Adolf Hitler
(1889–1945)

This chapter will explore the life and **legacy of one of history's most notorious dictators, Adolf Hitler.**

We'll look at sixteen facts about his rise to power, **anti-Semitic policies**, and **infamous death during World War II.**

470. **Adolf Hitler was born in Austria in 1889.**

471. **He became the leader of Germany before WWII** and wanted to expand German territory by conquering other countries.

472. **Hitler became a dictator who had total control over Germany,** its people, and its government policies.

473. **Hitler joined the German Workers' Party in 1919, and by 1921, he had become its leader.** In 1920, the name was changed to **National Socialist German Workers' Party** (or NSDAP, its German language acronym). **"Nazi"** comes from the pronunciation of **"National Socialist"** in German.

474. **During his time as chancellor of Germany,** Hitler started many programs that **improved industry and infrastructure.** However, he also spread fear among citizens, targeting those who didn't agree with him politically or whom he considered racially inferior.

475. **Hitler wrote a book called *Mein Kampf* (*My Struggle*),** which outlined his views on race and politics. **It was published in 1925** and became a **best-selling book throughout Europe** during the 1930s. However, it was later banned in multiple countries due to anti-Semitic and other hateful content.

476. **During his time as leader, he implemented anti-Jewish laws,** which led to Jews being persecuted throughout Europe and beyond during **the Holocaust**.

477. **Hitler's army invaded many European countries, including Poland, France, Yugoslavia, and Greece, between 1939 and 1941.** These conflicts produced devastating results, as millions were killed or displaced from their homes by war and genocide.

478. **Concentration camps were built across Europe,** where prisoners were sent to be worked as slave laborers or even killed for their beliefs or race. **Over six million Jews died because of Hitler's orders.**

479. **Hitler famously believed in something called *Lebensraum*, meaning "living space."** He wanted Germans to have more land by taking over other countries to access the resources they needed to survive economically.

480. **One of Hitler's most secret weapons during the war was a new kind of plane called the Messerschmitt Me 262,** which could travel faster than any other aircraft at that time.

481. **Hitler embraced new ideas of warfare,** which resulted in the famous German **"blitzkrieg"** ("lightning war") campaigns of 1939/1940.

482. **He ordered the construction of massive fortifications known as the Atlantic Wall** along the western coast of occupied France in preparation for a potential Allied invasion. This wall ultimately failed to protect the Axis forces from **this attack when D-Day** happened on June 6th, 1944.

483. **Hitler killed himself on April 30th, 1945.** He chose to commit suicide inside his bunker beneath Berlin rather than face capture or execution at trial after realizing his defeat was imminent.

484. **The Nuremberg trials** (1945–1946) held those responsible for **crimes against humanity** during WWII accountable, including sentencing Hitler's chief aides and followers to death or prison.

485. **Hitler is remembered today primarily as an evil man** responsible for many war crimes and atrocities against humanity during WWII, including **genocide and human rights violations** that led to millions of people's deaths.

Hirohito
(1901–1989)

This chapter dives into **the life and legacy of Emperor Hirohito,** who was the longest-serving monarch in Japanese history. **His reign spanned sixty-three years** and included some of Japan's most significant events, including World War II.

Let's explore fifteen interesting **facts about the emperor** who was forced to surrender after **the atomic bombs** were dropped on Japan.

486. **Hirohito was the emperor of Japan from 1926 to 1989.**

487. **He was born on April 29th, 1901, and died at the age of eighty-seven on January 7th, 1989.**

488. **His full title is Emperor Shōwa.** Shōwa means **"enlightened peace."** The emperor's name is given to an emperor after his death.

489. **Hirohito was a very important figure in Japanese culture and religion;** he was even believed to be an ancestor of the sun goddess **Amaterasu.**

490. **He traveled around Japan** extensively during his reign, visiting all forty-seven prefectures at least once.

491. **Before the war, Hirohito was awarded an honorary doctorate at Cambridge University in England.**

492. **After the atomic bombs were dropped on Hiroshima and Nagasaki, Hirohito announced Japan's surrender on a radio broadcast.** This was the first time the average person had ever heard an emperor speak in Japanese history. His address became known as **"Endure the Unendurable."**

493. **On September 2nd, 1945, Japanese officials signed the surrender** while aboard the USS *Missouri* in Tokyo Bay.

494. After WWII ended, **Hirohito spared many high-ranking military officers** from being tried as war criminals.

495. After WWII, other **Allied governments s wanted to try Hirohito for war crimes**, but the US government, especially **US General Douglas MacArthur,** who became the military governor of Japan, refused and asked him to help lead a peaceful transition toward democracy instead.

496. As part of postwar occupation by US forces, **Hirohito publicly renounced his divine status in 1946.**

497. Japan's government changed from a monarchy to a parliamentary democracy in 1947 with the new constitution written by American officials under **General Douglas MacArthur's** supervision.

498. During the last part of **Hirohito's** reign, **Japan recovered from the war** and became one of the most prosperous nations on Earth.

499. Emperor Hirohito loved marine biology and was an expert in the field. **He was a respected botanist** in his later years.

500. In 1972, Hirohito made the first Japanese state visit ever outside Asia when he visited the Netherlands with Queen Juliana aboard a luxury cruise ship called *Kashima* for a five-day trip.

Conclusion

As we reach the conclusion of **our exploration into World War Two,** it is clear that this period in history has left an indelible mark on the world. We have covered topics ranging from **the invasion of Poland to Joseph Stalin, Franklin D. Roosevelt,** and other influential figures involved in the war. We looked at the weapons and technologies used in **the war and the Nazi** concentration camps, where the true horrors of war took place. We saw how women and resistance movements aided in the war effort. We have gained invaluable insights into how this tumultuous period **shaped Europe and Asia** and changed global politics forever.

The Holocaust stands out among all these events for its sheer scale of cruelty toward humanity. Yet at the same time, there are stories of immense courage displayed by those who stood up against tyranny despite overwhelming odds. **Many bravely fought on battlefields** even when their own lives might have been lost.

Winston Churchill's words, **"Victory at all costs** ... Victory in spite all terror ... Victory however long and hard the road may be,"* echoes through history, as they are reminders of the courage and resilience that allowed humanity to overcome one of its darkest moments. **Recently, Ukrainian President Volodymyr Zelensky** has been compared to Churchill for rallying the Ukrainian people in their "darkest hour" and rallying much of **the world against the aggression of Russia.**

World War Two was a period of immense loss, pain, and destruction, yet out of this hardship emerged stories filled with bravery and hope for a brighter future. **It is our responsibility to remember** these lessons so we never repeat what happened.

Welcome Aboard, Check Out This Limited-Time Free Bonus!

Ahoy, reader! Welcome to the Ahoy Publications family, and thanks for snagging a copy of this book! Since you've chosen to join us on this journey, we'd like to offer you something special.

Check out the link below for a FREE e-book filled with delightful facts about American History.

But that's not all - you'll also have access to our exclusive email list with even more free e-books and insider knowledge. Well, what are ye waiting for? Visit the link below to join and set sail toward exciting adventures in American History.

To access your limited-time free bonus, go to: ahoypublications.com/

Sources and Additional References

1. "Warsaw Uprising (1944)." The Holocaust Encyclopedia, United States Holocaust Memorial Museum, 23 Sept. 2015, http://encyclopedia.ushmm.org/content/en/article/warsaw-uprising

2. Hochschild, Adam. "World War Two." Encyclopedia Britannica, Encyclopedia Britannica, Inc., 31 Oct. 2019, www.britannica.com/event/World-War-II#ref1039015.

3. "The Holocaust and World War II (1933–1945)." United States Holocaust Memorial Museum, USHMMorg Educators, www.ushmm.org/educators/learningactivitiesforlearnersandteachers#section5.

4. Roberts, Andrew, and Richard Overy eds., The Penguin History of the Second World War (London: Allen Lane/Penguin Books Ltd., 2001), 229–230, 232–233.

5. James Tarrant Jnr., Norway's Resistance to Hitler 1940 - 1945 (Oxford: Oxford University Press Inc., 2008), pp 13–14.

6. "The Battle of Britain 1940." The National Archives, www.nationalarchives.gov.uk/topics/world-war2/battle-of-britain/.

7. Lavery, Brian. "The Battle of Britain: A Turning Point in World War Two." History Today, 2 Sept 2011, www.historytoday.com/brian-lavery/battle-britain-turning-point -world war two.

8. "Women and the Battle of Britain 1940: 'Fairer Sex' Played Vital Role Too!" Historic UK, 9 July 2019, www.historic.uk.com/history-articles/women-and-the-battle-of- britain/.

9. "Pearl Harbor Attack: Summary & Facts." History, A&E Television Networks, www.history.com/topics/world-war-ii/pearl-harbor-attack.

10. United Nations. "The United Nations at a Glance." The Official Website of the United Nations, www.un.org/en/sections/about-un/the-united-nations-at-a-glance/.

11. Food and Agriculture Organization of the United Nations (FAO). "World Food Day" https://www.fao.org/worldfoodday.

12. "The Battle of Midway - WWII History." National WWII Museum, www.nationalWWIImuseum.org/war/articles/battle-midway/.

13. "Battle of Midway Summary." Encyclopedia Britannica Online Academic Edition. https://www.britannica.com/event/Battle-of-Midway#ref520206.

14. Harmsen, Peter & van der Vat Dan (2019). The Pacific War Companion: From Pearl Harbor to Hiroshima. Kindle Edition.